All Cooped Up

A Savvy Senior Society

Written by

Fiona Frizzle

And

Illustrated by

Tweetie Sweetie

Published in the United States of America.

Angelic Communications

Cape Cod, MA 02645

DRR

Digital Rights Reserved

ISBN-13:978-1979567305

ISBN-10:1979567301

"Feathers appear when Angels are near."

~Unknown~

We are Seniors

Impersonating Exotic Chickens

Impersonating Pincushions

Really?

This book is dedicated to the Senior Residents

of Pine Oaks III

Chickens in disguise

Preface

A book about chickens?

We were sitting together during our weekly Coffee Connection, when one of the women said, "This sounds just like a Chicken Yard." We giggled and agreed, that we did indeed sound like a bunch of chickens. "You should write a book about us chickens." Another said.

And so, it all began.

As resident author/publisher, I chose sixteen EXOTIC CHICKENS from the many breeds available on-line, because these women were not ordinary chickens. I printed the pictures for them to choose which one they wanted to Impersonate. They created the characters, giving each Exotic Chicken their own likes and dislikes, etc., but keeping their anonymity.

One of the women is a quilter, and created sixteen pincushion chickens, who then became the actual chickens photographed and illustrated in the book. Her husband, Big Bird in the book, created the coop (three wine boxes glued together).

Tweetie (her chicken name and illustrator/co-author of this book), also created added characters: Pierre the mouse, Reginald Racoon, Stinky the Skunk, Fernando el Zorro the fox who are the predators to the hen house. Oakee Dokee and Hoot, are the resident tree and owl. One more elusive predator is The Shadow, a Hen Napper with ulterior motives. Gobble dee Cook, Minnie Pearl, and Misty LaFogge are visitors to the coop, as is Santa Clacker, presents and Tinsel, a beautiful tree festooned with pearls and bunting.

The purpose of the book is to highlight the many conditions and situations that Seniors are facing today from medical benefits or lack of, to transportation issue and the surrender of their driving rights because of age, to the loss of friends, and so much more.

We are even forming a chorus, called The Cape Cod Chickies Chorus, and have a few plans. Yes, we will wear feathers.

Even though we are a small Savvy Senior Society, I believe we speak for all Seniors everywhere.

We are still young Chicks, and we are having Fun.

Happy Reading,

Fiona Frizzle.

Our Story Begins

The Chicken Yard

Somewhere on Cape Cod

An Early Summer Morning

CHAPTER ONE

The chicken yard was deathly quiet. We didn't have a rooster anymore, and hadn't for quite a while. We missed his melodious (well, not really) wake-up call. He was getting on in years, but that is another story. A bleary-eyed sun was struggling to push its way through the gray cloud cover. Typical Cape Cod weather, although today was going to be sunny and warm, according to Weather.com.

Where was everybody? Tweetie, an early riser, was usually out by now. No sound was coming from the roosts, either. *Are they awake yet?* I wondered, as I preened a few feathers, rubbed my beak, and adjusted my reading glasses.

The atmosphere in the chicken yard has been tense, extremely tense, these last few weeks. A few of the hens have become withdrawn and moody, worried. You can always tell, because their tail feathers were drooping. Not a good sign.

Although we aren't responsible for eggs anymore, (thank heaven for that) the younger hens now have that privilege. No one has any idea how painful it is to push those (Not Nice Words) things out. Small wonder we are always clucking. As for our shapes, laying all those eggs has raised havoc with our trim, beautiful figures. Once upon a time, we were slim and gorgeous, although still gorgeous, only in a slightly different shape. We are still prime, though, and our greatest fear is that we could be taken away any day for soups and stews. (Very FOWL) Personally, I think we are even too beautiful for that, but we never know.

We are all exotic breeds, you know, that is probably why they keep us around, because we are individually very different, and our plumage would add grace to any hen house, no matter how drab the coop may appear.

Our hen house, fortunately for us, is lovely, thanks to Lady Marion and Sir Lance-a-Lot. They keep our roosts in excellent shape. The grounds are pristine, the gardens gorgeous, flowers and plants surround us. Within the coop, when anything is broken or needs adjustment, it is taken care of at once.

Our feed is pretty good, a wholesome diet of pellets, mash, and herbs. I do so wish we had more vegetables, though, and fruit would be welcome, although chasing grapes around the hen house floor isn't always fun.

Wait! I think I hear someone. A sweet clucking reaches my ears. Its Tweetie. I thought it might be. She is the happiest hen in the yard. I don't think I have ever seen her sad, although she doesn't look very happy now!

The Chicken Yard

A few minutes later

Big Bird

Chapter Two

"Have you seen Big Bird?" she clucked worriedly, her large glasses bouncing down to the end of her beak, as she trotted over to me. She pushed them back up with a delicate prod from her wing.

Tweetie was a beautiful Silver Laced Wyandotte, her white, black, and gray feathers created an intricate and speckled body pattern right down to her gray under fluff (bloomers), and black short tail, which had a no-nonsense sway when she strutted away after making a well-meaning statement.

"Not this morning." I replied, "No one is awake, yet. Probably the after effects from that barbecue last night."

"I know, everyone was hiding under their straw nests yesterday afternoon, scared they would be featured on the menu. Most of them slept there all night." Tweetie clucked,

"They are all going to be pretty sore today, all cramped up, poor things. Should we get the walkers out?" I suggested. "Do you think they will need them?"

"I thought Big Bird was doing that." Tweetie sighed, "but I didn't see him in the storage shed."

"Did he go somewhere else?" I asked.

"He did say he wanted to go to one of the other hen houses up on the hill today to check out the two new baby bantams that just hatched."

"OOOH! Sweet." I cooed, as the Big bird in question came strutting merrily down the hill. True to his name, Big Bird was a handsome New Hampshire Red, His comb was a brilliant ruby, body feathers russet with gold tips, and his tail feathers iridescent black with cobalt blue highlights.

"Mornin', Chickies," he winked at us. "Big Bird's m' name and chicken's m' game!" he teased, winking broadly at Tweetie.

We had heard the line many times before, but it still made us giggle. He leaned over and patted Tweetie on the back. He was devoted to her, and had been for many years.

"How were the bantams?" I asked to give Tweetie time to compose herself. Her relief was clear. I think that barbeque had upset everyone.

"Cute little buggers, running everywhere. Their Mama was having trouble keeping up with them. Imagine! Twins are not very common here."

"Sounds like everyone's waking up." I said as strains of Hen House Blues started blaring over the speakers. Most hen houses have a rooster for their wake-up call. As our rooster was put in a fricassee a few years ago, Sir Lance-a-lot devised this method to roust us out of our fluffy, comfortable nests.

Still the chicken yard

Chicken Little

Chapter Three

"A-NU-ZZER BAR-BE-QUE, A-NU-ZZER BAR-BE-QUE", Chicken Little frantically blurted out as she came waddling down from the coop into the hen yard. "I hear zem talk-ing about it last night," her French accent obvious, especially when she was agitated or upset.

"How did you hear this bit of information?" Tweetie asked.

"When I was hiding un-dare my nest." She answered. "I was trying to be falling asleeps."

"Oh, Chicken Little, you're always thinking the sky is falling!" cackled Jollie Joan. "It never is, you know. You just get so worried, always thinking the worst, but your fears are unfounded. I know you are only thinking of the rest of us." She waddled over and gently patted Chicken Little on the back. "There, there, poor dear, don't you worry."

"Non, non, I deed hear zem saying wouldn't it be nice if zay could do deese every week. I did hear zem." Chicken Little declared emphatically, her wattles shaking, her tail feathers fanning out behind her. She was a Silver Laced Wyandotte, same breed as Tweetie, except that her feet had beautiful feathers around her ankles, probably due to her aristocratic French Heritage.

"OOOOOOOH, Dear!" Everyone said together. "Oh, my, oh, my, oh my." They all began to cluck worriedly, milling around in circles.

"This is not good, this is not good! This is not good!" Ms. Frazzle Dazzle clucked as little Ms. Unpredictable, usually called Missy, clung to Frazzle's wing. "I cannot spend another night hiding under my nest. There simply isn't enough room for Missy and Me under there."

"Somebody had better come up with a plan, then." Jollie Joan said. "Nurses always have a backup plan. They always know how to handle emergencies." She cackled. "They are trained to know what to do."

All eyes, beaks and cockles turned to look at her, waiting.

Jollie Joan

The Chicken Yard

Later that week

Tweetie Sweetie

Chapter Four

"A back-up plan?" asked Tweetie, as she waddled with Jollie-Joan out of the Coffee Clacken room into the yard. "How are you gonna do that?"

"I have no idea," sighed Jollie Joan, "What am I gonna do?"

"Well, I wouldn't worry too much, you know how forgetful they are." Tweetie consoled her, "They probably won't remember they even thought about needing a back-up plan." She patted Jollie-Joan on her wing, which was an odd thing, because it was usually Jollie who did the nurturing. "It might be a better idea to find out if the Owners are really going to have a barbeque each week before we run around like 'chickens who are gonna have their heads cut off'." She paused, removed her glasses, and started to polish them. "No pun intended."

"How can we do that?"

"I'll put Big Bird on it. He was in Army Intelligence. He can do some RECON." Tweetie smiled, nodded, and pushed her spotless glasses back up on her beak.

Jollie Joan was visibly relieved with this idea, as her tail feathers perked up and her wattle colors returned to normal.

"Come on, lets head over to the big coop" Tweetie suggested, and stopped as they heard someone clucking from behind.

"Did you hear about the Pot Cluck supper next Saturday?" Goldie, who was always interested in food, asked as she caught up with Tweetie and Jollie Joan.

Jollie dug her ample wing in Goldie's side and clicked in an undertone, "Tweetie is the one who organized it."

Goldie was a gorgeous Polish Hen with enormous head feathers. She went to the feather dresser frequently to keep them fanned and flossy. She had more of a public life than most of the other hens,

"Oh, I forgot," she clicked apologetically without pausing for a breath. "Well, I'm bringing this delicious vegetarian dish, everyone will love it." She clucked sweetly, "what are you bringing?"

"I'm not sure. Probably a mealy worm dessert, or maybe some oyster shell cakes, or perhaps a corn husk bread, or I might bring this new recipe I found for mash mush." Jollie-Joan clucked. "I'm sure I can come up with something. I used to cook all the time, that was before when I had a huge family of chicks, now, it's only me, so I don't do a lot of cooking, just eat whatever they feed us."

"What about you, Tweetie?" Goldie clucked, preening her head feathers.

"A mysterious mélange." Tweetie mumbled.

"What is that?" both Goldie and Jollie-Joan clucked together.

"It means, I have no idea."

"Attendez-vous! Attendez-vous!" Chicken Little came clucking up from behind them.

"Ziss Potting Cluck, how does one do ziss?" she clucked loudly so that the entire chicken yard could hear her. She caught up with the other hens and looked at them expectantly.

"It is very simple," Goldie clucked, explaining, "Everyone who wants to come brings a dish of food to share."

"Zen, I should dig in zee compost pile and fill a dish to bring?"

"You could do that," clucked Goldie, "but everyone else is cooking something."

"But of course," Chicken Little clicked back. "I shall cook somezing very French, then, and everyone will love ziss." She waved her wing in dismissal, and waddled her way back to her roost, clucking loudly in French, which none of the other hens had the least idea what she said, as they watched her leave.

"By the way, what do you think of our new Cluck-Cluck Timed automatic door opener for our coop?" Tweetie asked.

"It is wonderful, where did the Owners find it?"

"Big Bird said they found it on the Internet at www.cluck-cluck.time.hen

"I don't care where they found it, we are lucky to have it. I had to use the facilities early this morning." Jollie-Joan clucked her approval.

"Me too," said Goldie. "Amazing innovative technologies, now. Back in the day," She started to ruminate, and take another trip down Chicky Lane, "you had to hold and wait, egg coming or not!"

"We certainly have seen a lot of changes in our lifetime." Clucked Tweetie

"Most of them have been good for everyone." Goldie preened her head feathers again, "I wouldn't want to go back to the early days."

They all agreed to that, nodding their heads in unison.

"Well, Chickees, I have to get back to my nest, I just started a new feather quilt for a holiday gift. See you later." Tweetie waddled off wondering what innovative technology was in store for them now.

The Hen House

The Next Night

Sassy Sue

Chapter Five

All was quiet in the Hen House that night. The moon, almost full, gave eerie lighting inside the coop with its fragmented windows dusty with grime from months of neglect. The Owners had been entertaining guests all summer, as permanent residents of Cape Cod often do, because family and friends vie for weekends and weeks of visits so that they may also enjoy the sand, ocean, and sunny vistas of this precious peninsula.

The hens, tired after a day of showing off for all the visitors, were anxious for their beds. After being assured that the barbeque tonight was sea and surf, and that there was no chicken on the menu, not even egg salad, they had settled in earlier than normal. Their gentle snores were softly coordinating with each other.

Satisfied that all the hens were asleep, a little brown figure with enormous whiskers and a long curly tail, slid through a tiny hole in the side of the wall near the floor. He stood on his hind feet and cautiously sniffed the air, his whiskers vibrating with the cadence of each breath. His little button eyes scanned again from corner to corner, looking for any morsel of food he could find. He was VERY hungry, and hadn't found anything to eat for days.

He could smell food, he was certain, but there was none on the floor of the hen house anywhere that he could see. *Where could it be,* he wondered. His sense of smell had always led him to food, it never failed. *I don't see a crumb,* he thought. Following his nose, which was long and had a little black bulbous ball at the end, he also had HUGE WHISKERS. Stealthily, he crept all around the perimeter of the room, not making a sound.

NOTHING.

I smell food, I know I'm not wrong, he thought. *Perhaps it is up higher.*

Deciding that was worth a try, he crept slowly up the ladder that led to the nests, his tiny feet moving soundlessly, the smell of food growing stronger. He eased himself along the board that held the nests, delicious food smells guiding him. He inched his way to a large nest where the scent of food was powerfully strong.

OH, OH, PROBLEM, he thought.

There in the darkness he saw an enormously bulky Blue Orpington Hen was sleeping, her quiet snores and breath ruffling the feathers of her ample bosom. His bulbous nose was twitching VERY FAST. BINGO! The food was here, he was sure of it because the delicious odor of cheese floated delicately under his nostrils. He didn't see any cheese. Where was it?

Sniff, sniff. Light Bulb! It was under her and all her feathers. He could smell it; his nose was never wrong.

He started to drool and smack his lips, but stopped himself just in time. He didn't want to wake her up. That would be disastrous! *How am I going to get the food? I need a plan, but first I need to explore my options.*

Holding his breath, he inched his way around the hen to see if he could reach the cheese (that's what he was sure the food smelled like) more easily.

No, he couldn't see any way he could get at the food from that angle. Her feathers as well as her ample body were hanging over all the edges of the nest. BUMMER.

He strained his neck to see if there was an opening at the back of the nest under the hen, and all that hay.

Nope.

I need another plan.

What if I tickled her nose and made her sit up?

No, too risky.

He sat down on the edge of the nest to think. Just as he was deciding on his next move, a LARGE, ROUND, BEADY BLACK EYE opened and looked down at him. Then the head turned and the other LARGE, ROUND, BEADY BLACK EYE opened.

And from there it all went downhill.

Chapter Six

PIERRE

Bonjour! Oui, I am a mouse. Je m'appelle, Pierre

What can I say? I roamed into the Hen House one night looking for cheese. That was a near disaster, as I woke up all the hens. Wow! Did they scream. I have nevair heard such a Cackling!

Anyhow, when they finally calmed down, I explained how hungry I was, and hadn't eaten for a few days, and they were so KIND. You have no idea how much food is hidden in their nests for midnight snacks.

It is not necessary for me to tell you that I am now a full-fledged member of their coop. Of course, I am living in a little burrow outside the fence, but they leave scraps for me every day and I am never hungry any more.

Honestly, these hens are the nicest I have ever met. I've lived in France most of my life, and have travelled to many of the Provinces. When that became boring, I went in search of some adventure. I hopped a freighter and landed in New York. I hated New York, the people there were so self-absorbed, and the food was – um --
-fast.

So, I headed north to where the people were friendlier, and the food was tastier. I ended up here on this place that is called Cape Cod. It is a dream come true. It is very much like my favorite place in France, the French Riviera.

The Coffee Clacken

The following week

Ms. Frazzle Dazzle

Chapter Seven.

"Did you hear the news????" Ms. Frazzle Dazzle
clucked, fluffing her iridescent blue fuzzes, and
settling her tail comfortably. Ms. Frazzle was a
Blue Polish Frazzle chicken with gorgeous azure

blue feathers, a soft burnished gold collar and a flowing feather hat.

"What news?" asked the other hens as they sat together during their weekly Coffee Clacken.

"We're getting a POOL!"

"Really?"

"Are you sure?"

"Who told you?"

"I heard the Owners talking about it yesterday. They were down by the fence pointing and drawing diagrams." Ms. Frazzle Dazzle clucked earnestly.

"Oh, my, could this be true?"

"It would be WONDERFUL!"

"Can you just see us doing the back stroke or the breast stroke?"

"Just to dip my feet in would be marvelous, my bunions would love it."

"It's been so hot, even our feathers are sweating."

"Did you hear them say when this would happen?"

"Only that it would arrive sometime today."

"That soon?"

"Then it won't be an in-the-ground pool."

"The Owner was pointing and waving his arms."

"Oh, an Olympic Pool."

"Do we have any water wings?"

"Why?"

"I can't swim."

"Missy loves to swim."

"I love to dive."

"Will it have a deep end?"

"Where will they put it?"

"Over by the compost pile?"

"Not enough room there."

"This is a dream come true."

"We can finally cool off."

"All I can do is the chick-paddle."

"Will the other hen houses share it?"

"What about the baby chicks?"

"They will have a baby pool for them."

"Chickies, Chickies. Let's think about this," clucked Tweetie loudly to be overheard above all the cackling.

Instantly, all beaks were turned towards Tweetie and all eyes focused.

"You are certain this is what you heard, Frazzle?"

"Positive." She clucked emphatically.

"Then we better get busy and clean up the yard."

"What if they put it outside the yard?"

"It may not even be for us."

"No, the Owner was pointing to our yard."

"Wait, I hear a truck outside. It's in the parking lot."

All the hens quickly waddled over to the window to see if there was a truck in their yard. Anyone looking at the hen house at that time would have been very surprised to see Twelve sets of beady black eyes looking curiously out of the big coop window, beaks pressed against the glass, tail feathers up, wing on hips (really?) and a few chicken toes tapping impatiently trying to get a better view.

Anyone in the Coffee Clacken room would have doubled up in giggles to see twelve chicken bottoms, fluff showing (their bloomers), tail feathers erect, and twenty-four chicken feet tapping impatiently vying for a better position, all this crowded around a long narrow window,

The truck in question was a large white van which was already parked in the parking lot with PLUCKY POOLS written on its side in large ocean green letters.

"Oh, my!" the hens all clacked in unison.

"See, I told you."

"How exciting!"

"We really are getting a pool!"

"I can't wait to dive in."

"Will the water be heated?"

"I prefer chilly water myself."

"Oh, this is wonderful!"

"I don't care what the water temperature is."

"I love to swim in any water."

"Will we have lounge chairs?"

"And umbrellas?"

"And little tables for our drinks?"

"I can bring my book."

"I can sit and knit."

"This is too exciting."

"Look, they are unloading several huge boxes."

"They are carrying them around to the back, right to our yard."

"I am so excited."

"Let's finish our coffee and clear the tables."

The hens waddled away from the window and back to their seats, coffee cups waiting. One of the hens had brought a mealy worm snack this morning. That was hastily eaten, coffee cups drained, rinsed, and loaded into the dish washing machine. They were so anxious to get back to the yard to see what was really happening.

"I'll sweep the floor." One of the hens volunteered.

"We can get our mail on the way."

"Clever idea."

"Aren't you excited?"

"Yes, I really am."

"I wonder what it will look like?"

"Do you suppose they have it all set up by now?"

"Will it be full of water?"

"Can we swim right away?"

They waddled, clucking happily together along the walkway into the chicken yard where they (all 12), came to an abrupt stop. There in front of them, beautifully placed in the center of their yard was their gorgeous POOL!

Was that a picture of a large yellow chicken from some children's telly program plastered along the outside? Wondered Tweetie.

The Chicken Yard

Two nights later

Stinky

Chapter Eight

The pool, smallish as it was, was a most popular

place, visited constantly by the hens all day long.

The water was warmed by the sun, and the owner

kept it clean, refreshing it several times during

the day. They were in heaven. They had it all,

free range food, mealy snacks, a compost to dig in and now, their very own pool

All that pool activity wore them out, though, doing the chicken-paddle and wading in and out, as space allowed. There were no quarrels as to who could swim next, all the chicks were courteous and took turns. They swam, clucked, and dried off hanging their towels on the little line one of the hens had thoughtfully strung up between the house and a tree.

By the time the sun was dipping low behind the trees surrounding the yard, twelve tired hens were heading into the house, climbing the ladder up to their nests, to snuggle down in their beds expecting happy dreams.

The moon was in its last quarter, so the light reflected wasn't too bright, but bright enough to illuminate a path for another visitor to the Hen House. This was becoming a very popular place.

His fur was dark so he did blend into the shadows, except for the white streak of fur down his back and along his tail. He was a young little one, with a sweet disposition, shy with strangers, and tonight, he was VERY THIRSTY.

He had seen the pool full of water earlier as he ambled outside the yard along the fence. Tonight, and he was going to get – just a tiny drink. He was certain the hens wouldn't miss – just a tiny bit of their water. He ambled back and forth along the fence until he found the hole that had been dug there by some other predator. He looked around carefully before burrowing his way under the fence through the dug-out hole. *This might be a threat to the hens*, he thought, as he scrambled through up into the yard. Young though he was, he knew about hen-predators, and he was careful, because there might be a trap somewhere. Some farmers set them to catch intruders in their hen yards, and he was an intruder right now, after all.

He ambled over to the pool, now fully illuminated by the moonlight, his white stripe glowing, his darkness hidden in the shadows. Another look around to see if anyone was watching. He didn't see or sense anyone, so he leaned in to take a drink.

The water was delicious, cool, and refreshing. He drank deeply, satisfying the thirst that had brought him here, except, now he was hungry, very hungry. It had been an entire day since he had eaten anything, and his tummy was roaring, well, not exactly roaring, but gurgling because of all the water. He took a few steps away from the pool and his tummy gurgled some more. More steps, more gurgles. *This was fun*, he decided, as he danced and gurgled a few more times in the moonlight.

I wonder where the food is? he thought looking around the yard. There on the other side was a large pail with a tray. He ambled over to investigate, sure enough it was full of pellets, his very favorite other than dog crunchies, which he had found a few days ago in another yard a few houses away. Beside the pail of pellets was a half-eaten cabbage. He drooled. This was a feast indeed. Settling down he helped himself to pellets and nibbled on a leaf of cabbage, hoping the hens wouldn't mind. He ate until he couldn't manage another bite, and feeling very sleepy, now, he decided to curl up and take a teeny tiny nap.

It was almost dawn when Big Bird decided to check out the chicken yard. He considered this as one of his duties, although no one had ever told him to do it, but his days in Intelligence doing RECON made him very diligent. After all, he chanted quietly to himself, "Big Bird's my name, Chickens my game." And he meant every word. These chickens were his 'game'. It was up to him to watch over them, protect them, and keep them safe.

He wandered into the yard, looking around cautiously checking the little security system he had installed, unbeknownst to the Owners and the hens. That was when he spied the little ball of black and white fur over near the pail of pellets.

"Well, well, what have we here?" Big Bird clucked as he walked over to the little fur ball all curled up snoring away. As he reached down to touch it, the ball uncoiled itself and jumped, startled.

"Easy boy, easy. I'm not going to hurt you, stay still and we can have little chat." Big Bird folded his wings tightly against his chest letting the little fur ball know that he wasn't going to touch him or hurt him in any way, and hopefully avoiding a spray.

The skunk looked up at the HUGE chicken standing over him and gasped.

"I promise I didn't eat too much of the hen's food. I was very thirsty and very hungry." The skunk said, his little pointy teeth chattering.

Big Bird smiled down on the skunk. *He certainly is a cute little bugger.* He thought.

"What's your name, little fella?"

"Stinky."

"Well, Stinky, where do you live?"

"Nowhere." Replied Stinky, "I'm trying to hide out somewhere, the Animal Control is trying to catch me."

Hmmmmm. Thought Big Bird.

Oh dear, I am in trouble now. Stinky thought.

"How would you like to live here?" Big Bird clucked, a plan forming in his sharp mind.

"Here? Really?" Stinky replied, a plan forming in his little sharp mind.

"Yes," clucked Big Bird, "you could guard the yard and the fence when I'm sleeping.

"Wow! That would be easy." Stinky answered and thought of something. "Do you know, there is a hole in the fence over there, and a tunnel dug under it?"

"So that's how you got in. A leak in my security system, I guess."

"Sorry, Sir, just thought you'd like to know."

"Glad you told me." Big Bird clucked. "If you live here, you would have to live outside the Hen House. The hens wouldn't like it if you lived too close. By the way, why don't you smell like other skunks?"

"Arm and Hammer Deodorant. I found one in a trash pile, so I tried it. It really works."

"Ingenious as well." Big Bird clucked. "The wake-up call is about to go off. Come on, I'll show you the little box where you can camp out. I'll tell the hens about you and you can start working tonight. I've seen signs of a racoon and a fox lately."

"Really?" said Stinky. "Foxes and racoons don't like me at all."

"Precisely!" clucked Big Bird, his beady eyes gleaming, as he led Stinky over to a small empty box half-hidden outside the coop.

STINKY the SKUNK

Yes, I'm a SKUNK, but I don't smell, at least I don't think the hens can smell me. Probably because I use a very strong deodorant.

I snuck into the coop one night, not to steal eggs, because there weren't any, these were older hens, but to find a hiding place. Animal control was after me. When I explained my plight, Big

Bird agreed to allow me to stay, but not in their coop.

He found a little box outside the hen house, which is where I live. I eat the vegetables and any pellets the hens don't want, and I stay hidden during the day, so the Owners don't see me.

In exchange for my 'room and board' I keep the racoons and foxes away from the coop, and any other predators that may decide to stop by.

I am thinking of inviting my Mother to come and stay with me. She would fit right in with the hens here. She loves to knit.

Stinky and his Mom

The Chicken Yard

The next week

Oakee Dokee and Hoot

Chapter Nine

"The leaves are starting to turn." Gadget clucked sadly, as she stirred her coffee at the weekly morning Coffee Clacken.

"I noticed them, too." Ruby replied.

"Soon we will have to fluff our feathers before we get off our nests just to stay warm." Sassy Sue tutted.

"Who's fluffing their feathers now?" Goldie inquired as she came through the door.

"Welcome Goldie! Glad you're here. Where have you been?" asked Tweetie, as she pulled out a seat and motioned for her to sit.

"Over at the C. O. A." Goldie replied.

"The Council on Aging?" Ruby clecked.

"No, silly, at the Chickens of Age, a new benefit division especially for us." Goldie answered.

"Imagine that." Clucked Ruby, nibbling on the ground oyster shell cake Tweetie had baked that morning.

"I had an appointment to update my benefits." Goldie told them, stirring her coffee. "They have all these new benefits for us now. I saw an ad on the internet, and on T.V."

"Really? Do we need more benefits?" Ruby cooed, interested. "We already have our very own Feather Fallout insurance policy, and a Withering Waddle policy. The new Broken Beak policy was something we all needed, and our Happier Hearing benefit was a great add-on. I'm satisfied with the ones we have."

"Well, these new benefits are benefits for the benefits' benefits we already have. It's amazing."

"How much do all these benefits', for the benefits', benefits cost?" clucked Tweetie, very interested now.

"They told me that there were zero monthly premiums." Goldie clucked gleefully.

"Sounds like another too good to be true." Ruby tutted, skeptically.

"Did you sign up for it, Goldie?"

"Of course not, I told them I would think about it." Goldie answered. "It was too overwhelming for me to decide then."

Everyone nodded and clicked in understanding.

"Did anyone see the racoon out by the fence this morning?" Gadget asked as she took a bite of the mealy worm brownie that Sassy Sue brought to add to the morning snacks.

"Oh, no! not a racoon, again. That one last year really caused havoc in the other hen house up on the hill."

"This one will not be visiting anywhere for a long time. Stinky gave him a greeting that he won't forget for a while."

"Poor racoon." Gadget clucked. "He was only checking things out."

"Well, Big Bird employed Stinky to keep the Coop free from predators. That's why we share our pellets and water with him."

"He was only doing his job."

"Did anyone notice that Stinky doesn't stink?"

"Yah, that's strange. Wonder why?"

"I heard he uses Arm and Hammer deodorant."

"No! Really?"

"Well, whatever he does, I never smell him. And he is really cute."

"Big Bird put him in the little guard house. It's a perfect size for Stinky."

"Have you noticed our little tree in the corner of the yard? Some of his leaves are already turning such pretty colors."

"I saw an owl in that tree a few days ago." Tweetie finished her coffee and started to bring her cup into the kitchen. "Did anyone else see it?"

The other hens shook their heads, their wattles swinging side to side.

"With the leaves starting to turn already, we should really start thinking about Halloween." Sassy Sue suggested.

"Shall we have a party for the baby chicks, or will their mothers do that?"

"Usually their mother hens do that, but we could still have one here for them, it would be so much safer for them to get treats here."

"We could decorate the coop really spooky; make little cheese cloth ghosts, and hang little chicken skeletons everywhere."

"There are some real spider webs in the hen house. We could use those."

"They could bob for corn kernels in the pool."

"And play hide and seek the ghost."

"And play Chicky-Chairs."

"And drink Pellet Punch."

"And eat lots of candy, like chocolate covered mealy worms."

"And chocolate covered eggs."

Six pair of eyes turned to the source of that statement.

"OOPS, sorry, wrong holiday."

They all giggled.

"Do we dress up for Halloween?" one of the hens clucked.

"Oh, yes, lets!"

"That would be such fun!"

"Well, it's almost lunch time. Let's clean up here and meet next week to decide that."

"Good idea. I'll sweep if you wipe off the table."

Reginald Racoon

Reggie

Blimy, I hope I don't have to meet up with that
bloody skunk again. Caught me by surprise, he
did. Whoosh and I smelled like a blooming race
horse after a fast race. He apologized later,
nice of him, not a bad chap, but just doin' his
job he says. I understands that one, but blimy,
I had to take five baths in tomato juice. I

smelled like a Bloody Mary for days without the celery stick, thank you very much.

Now we have a workin' relationship, so's I won't call the coppers when I sees him again. I stays on my side of the fence an' he stays on his.

(Cary Grant)

The Coffee Clacken

The Following Week

Halloween Disguises Spike and Fluffie

Chapter Ten

"Do you think anyone will know who we are?"

"Naw, they couldn't possibly guess."

Spike and Fluffie, dressed in their Halloween costumes, were toddling along through the chicken yard on their way to the Hen's Hangout where a few of the hens were in the middle of their Coffee Clacken.

They moved silently and cautiously, stopping now and then to allow another hen to waddle by.

"Freeze!" Spike clicked, as two hens approached on their way to the pellet pail.

They both stopped and stood statue like, as the two hens waddled by.

"Oh, look, how cute. Pumpkins." Clucked one of the hens.

"Adorable." Clucked the other in reply.

After they had waddled out of hearing distance, Spike said, "See, I told you no one would recognize us."

"Yah, but that was close." Clucked Fluffie, nervously.

"Come on, we'd better hurry before someone does realize we are really hens dressed like pumpkins."

They waddled along as fast as they were able, the costumes limiting their steps.

"Wait." Clicked Fluffie quietly as she tugged on her costume and stopped, her feet tangled in some sand. "I have to sit down here and rest." Fluffie moaned quietly.

"We can't stop here. We are right outside the Hen's Hangout!"

"Yes, we can, we have to. I can't go any further." Fluffie groaned as she lifted a foot to shakeout the sand. She sat with a thud.

Inside the Hen's Hangout there was a hush as Tweetie clucked the news to the other hens.

"I heard about it a few minutes ago."

"Were they certain there really is one lurking about?" asked one of the other hens.

"Yes, and the hens up on the hill are all upset because of the little chicklings."

"What can we do about it?"

"If you notice anything or anyone strange lurking about, get a message to Big Bird right away," warned Tweetie.

"What if one of us is kidnapped?"

"I honestly hope that does not happen, but if it does, we will make certain you are rescued. Between Big Bird, Stinky, and Pierre, that Hen Napper doesn't stand a chance. Big Bird has also enlisted the aid of the little Racoon, even if he does smell, which may be an ingenious idea."

"He would keep the Hen Napper away because he smells so bad." Clicked one of the other hens.

"What does he or she look like?"

"No one knows," answered Tweetie.

"It could be anyone," clucked J. J.

"Even one of us." suggested Gorgeous Gladys or G. G. for short.

"Don't be ridiculous. Why would we want to be hen nappers?"

"Now that's a good question."

"Wait!" Tweetie clucked quietly and held up her wing for silence. The other hens at once became quiet.

"I hear something outside the door. Hush!"

"I don't think it is the Hen-Napper, do you?"

"I don't know, but I think we better find out." Tweetie whispered.

The other hens, frightened now with growing uneasiness, perked their ears to listen, mounting terror spreading among the rest of the hens.

"Grab your spoons, Chicks, and let's check this out NOW!" Tweetie commanded.

"Should we get a message to Big Bird first?" clucked one of the other hens shaking, her feathers, which were fluffing like a kitten's fur, sensing danger.

"No time!" Tweetie whispered. "All right Chicks, let's get 'em!"

And six chickens stormed out of the Hen's Hangout armed with spoons, their wings flapping, wattles wattling, twelve big black eyes huge with purpose and determination, heading straight for the two pumpkins sitting right outside the door.

"Take that, you napper!" one hen clucked and whacked one of the pumpkins with her spoon several times, the pumpkin a/k/a Spike ducked to avoid the blows.

The other hens in hot pursuit began to beat on the two (innocent) pumpkins who were stunned, unable to even respond.

Big Bird, alerted by Stinky that there was a fight going on in the chicken yard, burst upon the chaotic scene and clucked in the loudest voice he could muster,

"STOP THIS AT ONCE."

All six hens and two very bruised pumpkins immediately stopped what they were doing.

"Anyone care to explain?" Big Bird asked.

Whereupon all six hens and two muffled pumpkin hens all spoke at once.

"Wait, wait!" Big Bird held up a wing. "One at a time, please. Tweetie? Would you like to begin?"

"Oh sure, it's always me." She began with one wing on her hip in a defiant stance, Big Bird just grinned. He knew her too well. "We were talking about the Hen-Napper, when I noticed a movement right outside the door. We thought that's who they were."

"That's when we decided to protect ourselves and the other hens, and capture them." One of the other hens clucked in their defense.

Big Bird nodded, his red comb bounced with hidden laughter.

"So, who ARE these two pumpkins?" Big Bird inquired, helping the two bruised and battered pumpkins upright.

"Spike and Fluffie! And we were showing off our costumes for the Halloween party. We didn't think we were going to be --- well, you know."

"Oh, Spike and Fluffie, we are all so sorry. We didn't mean to hurt you!" The hens, all contrite and feeling very guilty now, apologized profusely.

"If you will let us, we would like to take care of your cuts and bruises. It's the least we can do." Tweetie offered, apologetically. "Chickee's, get the first aid kit," she directed, scooped the pumpkins into the room, and settled them comfortably as the other chicks ran around trying to bandage their bumps and contusions, murmuring their apologies over and over.

Big Bird, seeing that this situation was well in hand, turned and left the hens to do their work.

Much later, limping and covered with bandages on their way back to their nest, Spike and Fluffie commended themselves on the fact that no one recognized them.

"I told you, no one would know who we were."

"Ouch, I never thought spoons could hurt so much."

"Me either."

"My eye is really sore."

"My head hurts, I have a headache."

"Me too."

"Spike," Fluffie stopped to rest for a minute asked, "what's a Hen-Napper?"

"No idea."

The Hen's Hangout

The Following Week

Gobble-dee-Cook

Chapter Eleven

Three exhausted hens were slumped in their chairs, valiantly trying to stay awake. The Halloween party from the night before was still going strong at 3:00A.M. this morning. These three hens had stayed to clean up after the baby chicks, and waited as a few unidentified hens (or roosters) in costumes had finally left. The older (?) revelers (whoever they were) had helped themselves freely to the adult punch and eaten most of the mealy worm treats and oyster meal cupcakes. All the tired little baby chicks in sweet adorable costumes, carrying their candy corn scratch bags, had been taken home by their mothers much earlier.

One of the hens, her head on the table, began to snore quietly and was nudged awake by Tweetie.

"Thank goodness that's over." Lady yawned and rubbed her beak.

"Who were those hens? Did you recognize any of them?" Jollie Joan asked.

"No, I didn't, and I was afraid to even ask them who they were because of the Pumpkin fiasco." Chuckled Lady.

"They sure ate a lot of food."

"And drank all of our punch." Tweetie added.

"I'm so tired, I don't care if I ever have another party." Groaned Jollie.

"Let's make a fresh pot of coffee, I could use a hot cup." Tweetie suggested.

"Is there anything left to eat?" Jollie asked.

"Food's all gone." Lady clucked sadly.

"Now that our Halloween party is over, what's next?" Tweetie asked.

"Thanksgiving!" answered both the other hens, and groaned thinking of all the work that would entail.

"OH, I had forgotten that comes so fast." Tweetie clucked, "in less than three weeks."

"Yah, and right after that is Christmas." Jollie Joan croaked, her head drooping back onto the table, barely missing her coffee cup.

"And then the New Year." Added Lady, her head joining Jollie on the table top.

And then he let-down." Jollie Joan whimpered from her almost prone position.

"Chickies, I know you are tired, we can discuss that later, right now we need to think about Thanksgiving." Tweetie suggested, pouring fresh coffee all around.

"Gracious, not another party." moaned Lady, raising her head slightly from the table.

"No, just a big dinner prepared by the Owners for us." Tweetie answered.

"Oh, now that is really nice. It was delicious last year." Lady answered, sitting up straight, fluffing her bosom feathers.

"Our friend, Gobble dee Cook, from New York, is coming to visit." Tweetie clucked happily.

"It's so nice when our friends and family come to visit. My two sisters are coming, also, just for a short visit." Lady cooed.

"Which ones?" asked Jollie, deciding her brief rest was over, sat up straight and picked up her coffee cup.

"Margaret T. Hatcher and Eggatha Christie. I can't wait."

"Your friend, Gobble dee Cook is a turkey, right?" Jollie Joan asked.

Tweetie nodded.

"Why is he coming here?"

"He comes here every year so that he doesn't end up in someone's oven or on someone's table as the main course. He hides out here." Tweetie answered.

"How will you hide him, so the Owners don't know there is a turkey here?" asked Lady.

"I quilted a cover for his tail feathers, so he looks like a hen without the bloomer fluff, of course."

That seemed to satisfy everyone, and they quietly sipped their fresh coffee and tried to stay awake.

"The Click Clack Cable bill went up again." Jollie clucked, slightly annoyed.

"I know, and they don't offer any programs worth watching." Lady clucked unhappily.

"I'm tired of watching NEN, the Nest Egg Network."

"Not many of us hens want to watch sports, sports, sports. Even Big Bird is tired of that."

"Can you imagine, they have added two new cooking shows: **Coq au Vin**, and **Cock a Leekie**. Gives me the shivers and makes my feathers fluff, I refuse to watch them."

"Do we really need the cable?"

"Can we refuse to pay for it?"

"I don't know. When I moved in, they told me it was a benefit and part of the package."

"Guess that settles it, then. I'm too tired to think about it anymore."

The hens' coffee was cold now, unpalatable. That's when they all agreed that a nice, hot cup just might keep them awake for a few more minutes while they finished clearing up and setting the room to rights. They poured hot, fragrant second cups and tried to stay alert. They leaned their wings on the table, and held up very tired heads, eyelids drooping.

"After the holidays, it is really dull and boring here. I always want to get away."

"Me, too!" clucked Jollie.

"I know, let's plan a trip." Lady offered.

"Clever idea. Where?" agreed Tweetie

"Anywhere where the weather is warm, with beaches and sand, and lots of sun." dreamed Lady.

"The Bahamas, Bermuda, the Caribbean, those all sound nice." Jollie agreed.

"It's much too expensive to fly. We have limited incomes, remember." Tweetie reminded them.

"What about renting a van or a bus?" Jollie suggested

"Now that would work. We can drive down to Florida." Tweetie, who drove a school bus when she was younger, agreed.

"Disney? Oh, that would be such fun." Dreamed Lady, enchanted with the idea.

"Sure, why not?" Jollie agreed.

"What would we do for money?" Tweetie asked.

"We could have a bake sale." Clucked Jollie, not very enthusiastically, her voice fading, her head drooping.

"Well, Chickies, I for one am very tired and need to sleep even for a few hours. Let's discuss this next week, so we can plan our holidays, and this trip." Tweetie clucked her head drooping.

"Okay." They all agreed.

"I'll load the cups in the dish washer." Tweetie clucked, gathering them.

"I'll sweep the floor." Lady offered, and went to get the broom.

"And I'll wash the tables." Jollie Joan grabbed the sponge and started scrubbing.

Hen's Hangout

Coffee Clacken

The following week

Yard Bird Chicken Plücker

Chapter Twelve

"Eet's here, eet's here. I told you. We're
next." Chicken Little ran into the Coffee
Clacken room, "I told you they want to put us on

the menu." She reeled around and fainted flat on the floor, both feet sticking up in the air. The other hens looked at her in pure astonishment.

"What's here?" clucked Tweetie, worried now, as the other hens were dangling smelling salts under Chicken Little's beak, trying to revive her.

"She was in the courtyard when we got a delivery from The Yard-Bird Chicken Plucker factory. They dropped off a huge box with this picture on the side." One of the other hens tried to explain.

Three more hens, anxious to see what the commotion was all about, saw the carton in the courtyard, ran into the room and fainted right beside Chicken Little. Now there were four pair of legs in the air and four hens prostrate on the floor, their fluff scandalously showing. (bloomers).

"Honestly," clucked Tweety, "what next?" she slapped her wing to her brow and looked unhappily at the four hens in dead faints. "Okay Chickies, let's get them on their feet and find the underlying cause of this."

"The Chicken Plucker is the cause." Chicken Little, now conscious and sitting up explained. "The Owners purchased a chicken Plucker and want to have us for Thanksgiving Dinner." She wailed, large tears sliding down over her beak onto her ample bosom.

"The Yard Bird company also sells other products," Tweety explained. "They also have pellet pails, and waterers." She looked at Chicken Little and clucked kindly, "Big Bird heard the Owners say that we were getting a larger new waterer, so we would have plenty of unfrozen water this winter. It has a small heater installed."

Chicken Little and the other hens, Breezy Brie, J. J., and Sassy Sue, finally out of their fainting spells, a fresh cup of coffee in front of them, clucked happily now that there was no longer a threat.

"They also bought us a new treat pod for veggies, lettuce and delicious fruit pieces with a bell on the bottom, so we know when it's been filled." Tweetie clucked.

"Oh, zat is so much better." Clucked Chicken Little. "Je suis desolee, I didn't investigate first."

"You know," clucked Tweetie wisely, "this is how rumors start. Hens in Chicken Yards are the biggest and best gossipers anywhere. Sometimes one little word said can be changed into a terrible, hurtful thing as it is passed along the gossip grapevine. How many of us have been hurt because a little word or rumor was started that wasn't true at all?"

All the hens nodded in agreement. Many of them had been the target of such stories.

"It's so much better to find out the truth before starting rumors." Tweetie clucked.

The hens readily agreed to that and settled around the table, sipping their coffee, looking for something to eat.

"Help yourselves to my newest bakery attempts and give me your opinion." Goldie asked as she set some delicious looking foods on the table.

The hens, now that the crisis was over, began to help themselves to the pellet patties and broccoli bread that Goldie had made that morning, assuring her that they were delicious and would probably help them gain a few pounds. "You know where." Piped up one of the hens. The other hens giggled.

"I need to schedule a ride for my beak sharpening appointment." J. J. clucked. "I used to be able to fly everywhere. I had my own Feather Frequency Flyer license, but had to give it up." She clucked sadly. "That was a very unhappy day for me."

"We can get you on the Chickee Chugger, all you have to do is call and give them your destination and time of your appointment. They will pick you up, take you there, wait for you and bring you back home. Easy!"

"I use them all the time when I have appointments. You will love them." Breezy Brie told her. "Here is the number to call."

"I'm starting to have trouble with my beak, lately." Clucked Sassy Sue, "Perhaps I had better schedule a ride, too.?"

Make haste to tell you that all hens wrote down the number of the Chickee Chugger.

"It's getting cooler, now, I need to find someone to take out my air conditioner," clucked Chicken Little, "We need a reparateur (a handyman) around here to help us with some of the things Sir Lance-A-Lot doesn't have time to do."

Most of the hens agreed. Removal and set up of air conditioners were an ongoing problem for the hens. The units were too heavy for the hens to lift and either store or take them out of storage. Some of the hens knew how to service their units, and helped each other with those technicalities.

"Okay, Chickies, could we discuss our after the holidays get-away?" Tweetie reminded them. "The holidays will be over before we can blink and we will still be sitting here. If we seriously want to do this trip, we need to create some ideas of how we can raise enough funds to rent a van and" Tweetie paused for a few minutes because she had been giving this trip a lot of thought.

"OR, something else," she clucked cautiously. She had given this 'trip' idea a great deal of thought, and wanted to see how the hens felt about it.

All eyes were on Tweetie.

"Wouldn't it be a better idea if we did something for other Seniors who won't have much of a holiday?"

"Like what?" the hens asked in unison.

"We always have a Christmas party, that's nothing new." Clucked J. J. who also paused for a moment deep in thought. "Wait, I have an idea! we could make little gifts for everyone. Some of us could bake oyster shell cookies and package them with pretty bows for gifts. Food is always good to give. I'll get that started." J. J. giggled. "This is so much more fun than taking a trip."

"Some of us could offer a Chick-A-Dee Sitting Service for the mother hens up on the hill so that they could do their Christmas shopping while we take care of their baby chicks." Sassy Sue suggested.

The hens thought that was a great idea and Sassy Sue offered to organize that.

"What about a cleaning service?" ventured Breezy Brie.

"Most of the Seniors already have that service," answered Chicken Little, "instead, what about a Tittle-Tattle Tea Time, you know, offering to sit and have tea or coffee and read the news to them or with them, or just sit and tittle-tattle."

"Great idea, Chicken Little. So many of our friends here rarely leave their little nests, that is a happy thought. Could you see who needs a visit and we can all help with that one." Tweetie clucked happily. "I'm beginning to think that this is really better than a trip." The hens agreed. "Any more ideas?"

"As you all know, I sing in a choir and we visit churches all over the Cape, especially at holiday time. Why couldn't we form a singing group of our own?" Goldie, who had been sitting quietly smiled and clucked, "we could start with singing Christmas carols. It doesn't have to be a huge choir, just a small group to get together and sing some of the beautiful songs of the Holiday. We could even visit other Senior Centers and Nursing Homes if we wanted to."

"OH, that is such an innovative idea." The other hens nodded in agreement, chatting among themselves. "It would certainly make other Senior Hens very happy."

"Especially if we sing off key." Giggled Jollie Joan.

All the hens giggled, and agreed that this was, indeed, a clever idea.

"A visit to the Alzheimer's home might be a place to begin." Suggested Tweetie.

"They love to listen to music." Clucked Sassy Sue.

"I'm really excited about this one." Clucked Goldie.

"What should we call this choir?" Jollie Joan asked.

"We could call it the Cape Cod Chickies Christmas Choir." Fiona Frizzle suggested.

Goldie

Hen's Hangout,

Coffee Clacken,

The following week

J. J. (Jucie Joycie)

Chapter Thirteen

"What happened to you?" Tweetie asked, shocked by seeing the bandages and the wing in a sling on J. J. Always the self-appointed Mother of the Hens, Tweetie immediately stood, and bustled out to the kitchen to get another cup for J. J. She filled it with the dark rich brew of coffee the hens loved, added three heaping spoons of sugar, the best medicine for someone in shock, and lots and lots of cream. She placed it on the table in front of J. J., and waited.

Sitting gingerly, fluffing her bottom feathers for a cushion because she was still very stiff, and sore, J. J. nodded her thanks, took a few sips, sighed happily, and began her story.

"I volunteered to be in the Chick-a-Dee Sitting Service. The Mamma Hen of the bantam twins needed a respite. She was trying to get a few hours to do her Christmas shopping. I offered to take care of them for her." J. J. stopped her narrative, and wiggled in her seat trying to get comfortable so she could sip her coffee. Her knees were still too sore to sit for long, so she stood awkwardly and sipped her coffee standing up using her left wing to hold the cup.

"When some of the other hens found out, they asked if I could help them, too. They told me they could go with Mama Hen and get their shopping done quicker to be back to relieve me. if they shopped together. So, I ended up with not only the bantam twins (who were a handful) but also ten other chicks. They were so adorable, and looked so sweet sitting under their Mother's wings, I couldn't say no." J. J. shifted on her feet trying to balance her cup. "I have to sit down. My feet are killing me, too. I am just not used to running after all those chicks. The bantam twins were playing catch with one of the eggs from some Mother's nest. When I reached up mid throw to save the egg before it hit the floor, I fell on my wing. Yes, its broken in two places." She reached for her cup and drained it. "Do we have anything stronger?" she clucked mournfully. "The pain meds are wearing off."

"Sorry, only more coffee." Tweetie said as she went to refill the cup.

"I feel so bad, because I suggested the service." Sassy Sue clucked apologetically.

"I still think it is a promising idea. I believe if we are going to take care of little chicks, we need to do it in pairs, so we have backup, and can help each other." J. J. clucked, "I think this service will really help the Mother Hens, not just for Christmas, but during the rest of the year, too.

Who doesn't love to read stories to baby chicks?" Sassy Sue asked.

"And cluck them to sleep." Tweetie chirped as she remembered when her baby chicks were sweet and cuddly. Truth be told, the rest of the Chickies were thinking the same thing.

"Has anyone done the Tittle Tattle Tea Time?" Gadget asked as she bounced into the Coffee Clacken room and hurried to the kitchen to grab a cup of coffee before it was all gone. "Because I would like to do that." She clucked, peeking around the door of the kitchen.

"Fancy Nancy has just returned from the spa. She was there for a long time with a broken hip, which we didn't know. Something about that privacy law that no one can get information about anybody unless it's approved by the patient. So, she was cut off from her friends here for all that time. Lady Marion would not tell us anything, not even where Nancy was." Tweetie clucked annoyed and sad. "She could use a Tittle Tattle Tea Time. We just helped her get settled back in her nest."

"I would like to do that, but I don't even know her. I just moved in from New York." Gadget clucked sadly.

"You're right, Gadget, some of the other hens can do that, or go with you and introduce you. I think Nancy would love that." Tweetie chirped happily.

Fancy Nancy

"Is it that late already?" J.J. clucked surprised.
"Thanks for all your support, and for the coffee
Tweetie." J.J. stood again ready to leave. "I
really need to get to my pain meds. See you
later." She hobbled to the door. "Maybe for
Trivia this afternoon if I don't fall asleep first."

The Chicken Yard

A few nights later

Fernando el Zorro

Chapter Fourteen

There was no moon this night, the sky was clouded over with threatening clouds. *It will rain soon*, he thought. The wind had shifted direction, and he instinctively knew that a change in the weather was coming. How long had he been running? Too long, if he was honest with himself. He was exhausted. Earlier, he had thought there would be no threat to his life here on this isolated arm of land sticking out into the ocean. It was almost an island. *How could they possibly find me.?* He wondered. *I am almost invisible.* He ran, not watching where he was going and bumped headlong into something.

"Ouch!" he yelped as he drew back to look at the wire fence in front of him. *I think this might be a chicken yard. It certainly smells like one. This might be a safe place. They will never think of looking for me here.*

He slithered along close to the ground, staying as close to the fence as he could, sliding from shadow to shadow until he came to a hole in the ground, and what appeared to be a tunnel under the fence. He lowered himself carefully into the hole, slipping easily through the hollowed-out rut. He was almost into the chicken yard, his head and shoulders rising at the end of the tunnel. He crouched down to get a full view into the yard. This was better than he expected to find. This was a chicken yard a la crème de la crème. *Did these hens appreciate what a gorgeous place this was?* He wondered. *I really cannot believe my luck.* He started to pull himself up out of the tunnel when he realized he was stuck, or something was stuck. *His tail! Darn!* He tugged and tugged, trying to yank it free. *I must be stuck on the fence somewhere. I can't go back and untangle it because I can't turn around in the tunnel. I can't call for help, either. Maldita sea, what a terrible fix, now what do I do?*

Fortunately, or unfortunately Pierre had seen the intruder slinking along the fence. He followed him, staying behind in the shadows making certain to stay hidden, which was preposterous, because he was a teeny, tiny mouse with big ears and a very long tail. He watched as the fox slid into the tunnel and Pierre scurried under the fence through his secret hole, and went to warn Stinky.

"Stinky, wake up!" Pierre whispered into Stinky's ear. "There is a fox coming into the yard."

Stinky uncoiled himself and blinked, trying to get his thoughts together.

"Where? When?" He whispered back rubbing the sleep out of his eyes.

"At the tunnel. He is there now."

Stinky stood and waddled out of his little box, and headed over to the fence, Pierre right behind him. There he saw the fox, half in and half out of the hole at the end of the tunnel.

The fox was stuck and at the mercy of this black and white bunch of fur, which he knew by instinct and his Momma's many warnings when he was a baby fox, that this was not going to be pretty.

"Caramba!" the fox whispered to anyone who would listen, hoping he could think of a way out of this situation. He clenched his eyes shut.

"Fox, this is a warning!" Stinky growled in his deepest voice. "Leave this yard at once!"

There was long dead silence as the fox was trying to think of what to say or do. Finally, he decided that the truth was always best.

"I can't!" the fox replied timidly, opening his eyes, "I'm stuck."

"Where?" asked Stinky, "you look fine from here. No excuses. Leave!"

"My tail is caught on the fence at the other end of the tunnel, and I can't turn around to untangle it."

Pierre tapped Stinky on the shoulder, "I'll go and check this out." He whispered, and scurried away to disappear under the fence.

"You shouldn't be here." Stinky pointed out to the fox. "Big Bird will really be upset if he finds you."

Pierre returned, and whispered to Stinky, "He's stuck all right. He has a very long tail."

"Can you untangle it?"

"Not without some help." Pierre replied.

"I'm sorry to give you so much trouble." Fernando whispered, trying not to lose his dignity and cry. "I have been running away all day."

"From who?" asked Stinky and Pierre together.

"Animal control."

Both Pierre and Stinky knew how dangerous that was, Stinky had been trying to escape from them, too, when he ended up here.

"Come on," called Stinky to Pierre.

"Where are we going?" Pierre asked as he followed Stinky out of the yard by the main gate because the tunnel was a little clogged right now.

"Where are you going?" whispered Fernando rather loudly.

"To free your tail. Don't move."

Fernando was relieved, but worried as to what would come after the freeing of his tail. He felt, rather than heard the two would be rescuers yank his tail and tug a few times, painfully, but at last he felt a final tug and he was able to pull his tail up to his body. He stayed still as a stone until he heard Stinky and Pierre slide up beside him.

"Thanks so much, guys. I am very grateful. By the way, my name is Fernando, who are you?"

"I'm Stinky and this is Pierre."

"Nice to meet both of you, I hope. Can I get out of the tunnel now?"

"Sure, and then we have to decide what to do with you." Stinky said.

Fernando gulped, because that was very worrisome. What could they do with him? Besides, he was hungry and extremely tired by now and all he wanted to do was to go hide somewhere safe and take a long nap.

"I can leave now if you want, but I would really appreciate a place to hide and sleep a little before I go. I am awfully tired, perhaps you might have a small bit of food, too?""

"The food's no problem, but the place to hide is!" said Stinky.

"I know," said Pierre, "we can ask Oakee Dokee or Hoot, they might know of a good place."

"Food first, while we go and ask Oakee Dokee and Hoot. Stay right here and I will get you something to eat. Pierre, would you go and wake Oakee and ask him about a place for Fernando to sleep? I'll be there in a moment."

Pierre took off and went over to climb up Oakee and wake him up. He clambered out onto a branch, shaking it so that some of the leaves fell. Oakee was still snoring gently, Hoot sound asleep in another branch.

"Oakee, wake up!" Pierre insisted, shaking the branch again, showering the ground with more leaves.

"I'm awake, what's wrong?" Oakee asked stretching his branches so that Pierre had to hold on for fear he would fall out of the tree.

"Oakee, stop stretching, please, and I'll explain."
He waited while Oakee stood still, his branches
steady, and the leaves stopped falling. Pierre
sniffed, his little black bulbous nose twitching as
he cleared his throat and began. "We have this
fox, you see, who is running away from the Animal
Control and needs somewhere to sleep. Can you
think of any place where we can hide him for a
while?"

"Hmmmmm, well, yes, I can. I have this hole in my
trunk near my roots that is covered with leaves
so no one can see it. Do you think he would fit in
there?"

"I dunno, let me go look." Pierre scampered down
off Oakee's branches and started to explore the
base of the tree. "Where is it?" he called up to
Oakee.

"Near the knothole to your left."

"WOW!" exclaimed Pierre, as he peered into the hole. "This is a perfect place. You don't mind?"

"Not at all," said Oakee, "it would be a treat to have some company for a change. Hoot is nice, but he is pretty quiet most of the time, except when he hoots in my ear."

"I'll go and tell Stinky." Pierre started to scamper away, when he thought of something. "Thanks, Oakee, we really appreciate you doing this." And he took off into the chicken yard to tell Stinky that Fernando had a safe place to hide for a while. Just in time, too, because it started to sprinkle.

Fernando el Zorro

Hola! I am Fernando the Fox. In Spain, I was a famous bullfighter with a special hide-away. When I went to England, they thought I was a fox for their hunt. They wanted to set the hounds after me and horses, too. Imagine that - to me a famous fox, el Zorro! It was degrading! Look at my beautiful tail, a fox tail worthy of a famous bullfighter. And my moustache! There isn't another fox who has such a moustache.

Here this won't happen because they will love me. The Hens will give me, Fernando, a safe Hide-Away, so these English men will not use me for their hunt.

The Skunk insists that I must still be on the outside of the fence, but that is a good place to be. I can help keep the Hens safe. After all, I was a famous bullfighter.

(Antonio Banderas)

Hen's Hangout

Coffee Clacken

Next Week

Fiona Frizzle

Chapter Fifteen

The air in the chicken yard was crisp and cool,
that reminiscent smell only Fall could bring.
Inside Hens Hangout, the fragrance of rich
roast coffee filled the air of the Coffee Clacken

room as several of the hens sat around the table discussing some of the local events. The door opened admitting another exotic hen, yellow feathers wafting in the breeze as she slipped into the Coffee Clacken room.

"Morning Chickies!" she clucked and plunked her purse on the table, and her feathers down on a chair.

"Fiona, good morning, we thought you weren't coming." Tweetie chirped. "Where were you?"

"I was over at C. O. A. (Chickens of Age), meeting with B. A. B.B.B. (Benefits are Bothersome, But Beneficial) trying to decide which supplemental insurance benefits I need. This is enrollment time and I have to decide before mid-December."

"How did that go?" Tweetie asked, interested because the other hens were listening attentively.

"They gave me several pamphlets to read and another appointment in a week so that they can get me started." Fiona told them. "All this research takes me away from my writing. It's Bothersome, no pun intended." She stood and went to get her cup and fill it with coffee, four spoons of sugar and topped it with lots of cream.

"Boy!" she sighed, "Do I need this," as she sat down with her brew.

"How is the book coming?" Ms. Frazzle Dazzle asked. (The book meaning the one Fiona was writing for the hens here in the coop.)

"It's almost finished, another two or three chapters, and then the ending. I am planning to have it published before the holidays."

"What if this book makes money? What do we do with that?" Tweetie asked.

"We can donate some of the profits to other chicken farms, or even to the food bank." Fiona suggested. "We don't have to worry about that right now, but it is something to think about."

"Has anyone seen or heard anything about The Hen Napper?" asked Breezy Brie.

"No, nothing." Tweetie replied, "Big Bird hasn't seen anything of him either,"

"Who's coming to Trivia today?" clucked Frazzle Dazzle, "I'm coming because I have been practicing."

"Good, because we need someone with the right answers. When is the tournament?"

"January or February, I think., replied Breezy, polishing her glasses, and setting them on her beak, "I hope we can win the trophy back this time. We lost by two points in the last tournament."

"That was sad, but they were really smart with the correct answers. That's why I have been practicing." Frazzle said.

"If everyone shows up this afternoon, we can begin on some different questions." Tweetie clucked, "I have new ones from an old Trivia game I found in a thrift shop."

"Is that legal?"

"I hope so, anyhow, the questions are from the last century. I can't see any conflict there; besides the old questions will sharpen our brain."

"Oh, that would be novel!"

"I have a pencil sharpener that will do that!"

"Chickies!" Tweetie intervened before this conversation got out of hand, "spread the word so that everyone will come. The more we practice, the better we will be."

"How are we ever going to be able to remember all those facts?" asked Breezy Brie, "I can't remember what I had for breakfast."

"Well, I have a lot of memory problems, but I have found that rehearsing with the Trivia group, even though we don't have all the answers, I am remembering more facts because we

practice together. I think that's a good thing."
Clucked Frazzle Dazzle.

"True, Frazzle, I think the group Trivia practice
will help us all." Tweetie clucked wisely.

"It's almost lunch time, we better clear up here
and see you all back at one this afternoon." Brie
stood and carried her cup to the kitchen with the
rest of the hens following.

Hen's Hangout

Coffee Clacken

The following week

Chickee Fillet

Chapter Sixteen

Running through the yard as fast as her little hen

feet could carry her, Chicken Little bounded into

the Hen Hangout gasping for breath. She stood at the door of the Coffee Clacken room as six other hens stared at her in astonishment and apprehension. Chicken Little certainly did not bear good tidings, especially now as her wings were flapping, and her beak was opening and closing rapidly, no sound was coming out. Her feathers were ruffled, standing straight out, and her ample bosom was swelling alarmingly as she tried to catch her breath.

"Chicken Little, come and sit down," coaxed Tweetie, pulling out a seat and gently moving the fluttering hen into it.

"Eet izz here!" Chicken Little finally gasped through wheezing breaths, "I saw it in zee Chicken Times, right on zee front page."

She was breathing a little calmer, now, so Tweetie asked Goldie to go to the kitchen and get a cup of coffee for Chicken Little. "Hot and sweet!" she called out as Goldie waddled into the kitchen, waving her wing as she went.

"Now, Chicken Little., tell us what was on the front page of the Cape Cod Chicken Times."

"Here it is." Frazzle clucked as she waved a copy at the other hens. "This is our copy."

"Look on zee front page!"

Frazzle and the other hens gathered around and looked at the paper. There in big bold letters was the headline:

CHICKEE FILLET COMES TO HYANNIS.

"See, I told you. Zay have even listed what they serve.

Chickee sandwich – 440 calories

Chickee deluxe – 500 calories

Spicy chickee deluxe – 570calories.

Zay have made us into calories and put us in an roulea d'oeufs." (egg roll)

Chicken Little rolled her eyes, became very pale (if a black and white speckled chicken could become pale), put her wing to her brow, swayed a little, muttered something in French, "OH, J' eperdu (distraught)!" and fell into a dead faint (again).

"Oh, dear, this may be more serious than we think." Tweetie clucked, "Someone read the rest of the article, please, while I try to revive her," and ran for the smelling salts.

"The article says that the owners of the establishment plan to use fresh chickens from local chicken farms." Goldie clucked, reading from the Times.

Three more chickens fell into dead faints, feet in the air.

"This is impossible!" Tweetie slapped her wing on her forehead, and tried to think.

"What are we going to do, Tweetie?" Goldie, the only chick not in a dead faint clucked worriedly, as she waved smelling salts under the beaks of the four hens upside down on the floor.

"I'm not sure." Tweetie answered vaguely, "we have to protect the hens. I don't have any idea how to do that, at least not yet."

"What if we dressed the hens up in disguises? No one would know who or what they were?" suggested Goldie, "I know where we can find fancy hats for the hens and lace scarfs and sun glasses. No one will recognize them."

"Will that be enough to deter Chickee Filet, do you think?" Tweetie chucked worriedly.

"I think so, and the hens will love it."

"Let's get these chickies on their feet and tell them our plan. I just hope it works."

"It will, I'm certain." Goldie clucked and went to find more smelling salts.

Hen's Hangout

Coffee Clacken Room

The Following Week

Chapter Seventeen

The Chicken Yard was quiet this morning, a few
of the hens were waddling about on their daily

chores, a little furtively because of the Chickee Fillet Fright. Several of them were wheeling little carts filled with bags of clothes on their way to the laundry room, others heading to the mail boxes, except for three hens dressed rather extravagantly. They were heading towards Hens Hangout to the Coffee Clacken room.

"Do you think anyone will know who we are?" clucked Gorgeous Gladys, nickname G. G.

"No, I doubt it. We are dressed rather differently. My own Mother wouldn't recognize me," Breezy Brie clucked prettily.

"Well, no one would recognize me at all," clucked Frazzle Dazzle, "this hat and sunglasses completely hide my beak and eyes."

The three chicks opened the door and swanned into the Coffee Clacken room smiling and giggling, confident that no one would recognized them, so they thought,

"Morning Frazzle, G. G and Breezy. Where are you going all dolled up?" Tweetie asked as she came out of the kitchen with a cup of coffee. She sat down at the table alongside Ruby and Goldie who already had their coffee and were helping themselves to some freshly baked worm muffins and lettuce leaf rollups.

"We are in disguises so that Chickee Fillet won't find us, Tweetie, I thought you knew we were doing that." G. G. clucked peevishly.

"Yah, it was your idea, wasn't it?" Breezy Brie chirped.

"Of course, it was my idea, but it was for when you left the yard."

"Well, we are leaving the yard because we're going to the other coops up on the hill to do some Tittle Tattle Tea Time. A few of the Momma hens are feeling poorly, so we thought we would cheer them up."

"Excellent idea, Chickies" Tweetie almost crowed her delight.

"How much longer will we have to stay in our disguises when we go out?" Frazzle asked.

"Until we are sure there is no longer a threat."

"Speaking of that, Tweetie, has anyone seen anything of the Hen Napper lately?" Frazzle asked.

"Big Bird said that Reggie the raccoon thought he saw The Napper the other night prowling around, but as he followed him, The Napper just disappeared into the shadows." Tweetie clucked, "So, be careful when you go out at night for any reason."

"Well, we won't be out at night, our Tittle Tattle Tea Time will be during the afternoon when it is still light." G. G. clucked.

The other hens agreed, and helped themselves to the broccoli bread and worm muffins.

"What are we doing for the Christmas Party this year? It is in less than two weeks. Will we have a Secret Santa Clacker?"

"Oh, yes, definitely. Remember to put your names into the basket for the drawing next week." Tweetie advised.

"Last year it was such fun. No one knew who gave what presents to who." Clucked Frazzle.

"So, how does this work?" clucked Ruby, who was not there last year, but on a visit to family at the Cackle Hatchery.

"We put our names in the basket, and next week Big Bird watches us as we take turns pulling a name out of the basket. That name is who you get a present for, you become their Secret Santa Clacker. If you get your own name, you have to put it back and Big Bird shakes the basket again." Tweetie explained.

"Okay, I get it!" clucked Ruby. "What fun, and no one knows, ever?"

"It is supposed to be a secret." Tweetie affirmed. "The party is in two weeks' time. Every hen brings a snack. We always have plenty of food, but we will have a sign-up sheet for you to give us an idea of what you are bringing." Tweetie continued. "Big Bird and I will provide the drinks."

"This sounds like lots of fun." Goldie clucked.

"Can we bring guests?" Breezy Brie asked.

"Of course," Tweetie clucked happily. "My cousin Minnie Pearl is coming."

Ruffle Ma Feathers

Nashville, TN

Two weeks before Christmas

Chapter Eighteen

Minnie Pearl

Hi Y'all! Ma name's Minnie, Minnie Pearl, and I'm Tweetie's cousin from Ruffle Ma Feathers down in Nashville. Tweetie and Big Bird have invited me to visit over the holidays, and that will be such fun. I haven't seen Tweetie for the longest time, because I have been on the road with the rest of the band singing in concerts. We're almost finished with this tour. Our last concert is in Boston, so I can easily come to the Cape. It will be such fun to catch up on all the gossip.

Tweetie wrote and told me that there will be other guests for this party, too, but she didn't say who they were, which is a little mysterious, but I do love a mystery. She did mention something about a Countess or something. I'm just dying to find our who this mysterious person is. Well, See y'all then. Gotta run, the boys are ready to board the bus.

Cluckingham Palace

England

Two Weeks Before Christmas

Misty La Fogger

Chapter Nineteen

Allo! Madame et Monsieur

Je m'appelle Misty, et I arrived in zee Chicken

Yard very late one night. I am zee cousin of zee

Chicken Little. She invited me to come and share in the holiday festivities, you know, the one that you call Joyeux Noel, to cheer me up.

I travelled from Cluckingham Palace in England where I was arranged to marry a Duke of Wingsate, but he had already found another bride, and so I was redun-date (how do you say it?) not needed anymore. So sad, and I even have on my newest little French chapeau (hat), which I carried all the way from France.

You can see that I am a Comtesse Stephanie Felicite Brouillard, named after my great grandmother who was the Comtesse de Genlis. I am 34th in line for the throne. I came here to escape such an unhappy arranged marriage. I use my sobriquet 'Misty' because I wish to still be hidden in the shadows.

Alors, I am here with zee Coeur Brise (broken heart). No one will love me pour toujours et a jamais (forever and always).

Excusez-moi, I must go quickly for the transport for the ocean liner is leaving within the hour and I must not miss it. My cousin will be waiting for me at the port of Boston.

Hen's Haven

Christmas Eve

The Party.

Santa Clacken and Tinsel Tree

Chapter Twenty

Hen's Haven was alive with activity, hens rushing everywhere setting up tables, chairs and finding room for all the presents for the Secret Santa to be held as soon as everyone was in the room, and Santa had arrived.

Tweetie was in the middle of all the chaos when the door opened, and Minnie Pearl came in. Tweetie rushed to greet her and invited her to come and meet the rest of the Chicks. Everyone was very impressed to meet a real-live singer from Nashville, and she was begged by most everyone there to please sing a song or two, which she did and was practically deafened by the applause and cheers. Hens can be boisterous.

The Haven settled down to await the much-anticipated visit from Santa, because then the presents could be distributed and opened.

There was a soft knock on the door. J. J. was standing right beside it, so she looked out to see Chicken Little and this other person waiting to enter. A hush fell over the room, as the other chicks knew something was happening. They were certain it was Santa, and began to move into the center of the room.

The door swung open, and Chicken Little escorted a gorgeous hen into the room. This Chick was dressed almost completely in white satin with a sprinkling of black beads across the front of her gown. She had long black softly curled hair with a streak of white, and had on a black velvet and lace train falling behind her. On her head was a sparkling diamond tiara.

Comtesse Stephanie Felicite Brouillard

You could hear a pin drop!

"Good Evening Everyone, may I present my cousin, Comtesse Stephanie Felicite Brouillard who has travelled from England to be here with us tonight. Please make her welcome."

No one moved. The silence became oppressive.

Tweetie stepped forward and bobbed a curtsy, held out her hand and said,

"Welcome to Cape Cod, Your Majesty."

"Thank you, you must be Tweetie?" Misty took Tweetie's hand and shook it gracefully.

Tweetie nodded.

"Please call me Misty, I do not wish to make zee fuss. And no more curtsies, s'il vous plait? I vish to be - how do you say - a-non-y-mous?"

The rest of the Hens laughed and assured her they would remember to call her by "Misty".

Everyone started milling about, chatting with each other, remembering to bring Misty into the conversations, and soon she removed her black velvet cape and relaxed.

There was a loud hammering on the door. Everyone froze, not daring to breathe.

"Well, if you don't want any of your presents, then I'll take off again." Came the cranky voice from outside the door.

"Santa!" everyone shouted and screamed. "Come in, come in!" and he was pulled through the door into the middle of the room.

"Now, that's better! I was beginning to think that you didn't want me to stop here this year."

Everyone laughed and shouted, assuring him that wasn't the case, and Santa just laughed and made jokes about it. He sat on the chair the hens had decorated especially for him, pulled his sack beside the chair, and began to call out the names on the packages, handing them over to the recipients.

The food came out then, carefully placed on the big long table against the wall, and everyone lined up and filled their plates. The hens found places to sit and eat, chatting to each other. Someone had rigged up a radio and added some seasonal music for the background.

All was happy in Hen's Hangout.

Hen's Hangout

Half an hour later

Stinky

Chapter Twenty-One

Another knock on the door, this time not as loud
as before, but loud enough so that Big Bird heard
it and went over to see who was there. It was
Stinky. *He would never come inside the coop*
unless something has happened. He thought.

Big Bird stepped outside the Hangout and closed the door quietly.

"What's up, Stinky?"

"So sorry to interrupt your party, Sir, but this is URGENT!"

"I'm sure it is, Stinky," Big Bird cucked calmly, "wanna tell me what's happening?"

"Well, Sir, we have The Hen Napper. Reggie is sitting on him and Fernando is holding him at sword point. We figured you should know."

"Where is he?"

"At the end of the tunnel, Sir, right where Fernando was before. We blocked the other end outside the fence, so he couldn't escape."

"How did you do that?" Big Bird asked, trying not to smile.

"Hoot, Sir, he is sitting on the hole. Pierre is helping him. They filled it with rocks and leaves."

"I better go and take a look." Big Bird headed out of the Hangout over to the chicken yard, Stinky right behind him.

It was dark, but the moon was filtering between the clouds enough to light up the scene before Big Bird. There they were, Reggie was sitting on top of this white and black chicken who was lying very still, because Fernando had him at sword point, aimed at his neck. The Hen Napper's black hat had rolled away, and his black cape was crunched up underneath him. He still had his sunglasses on, even though it was very dark.

"So, you are the elusive Hen Napper." Big Bird clucked

"Yes, Sir, I mean no harm to anyone." He choked out, the sword point dangerously close to his chin.

"Why are you lurking around our chicken yard, then?" Big Bird clucked again, only his cluck wasn't a happy one.

"I'm awfully lonely, Sir. I just want to find someone to love, and who will love me back. I have been looking everywhere in chicken yards all over the Cape." The Napper said sadly.

"What makes you think you can find the love of your life here in this chicken yard?"

"Sir, these hens are so happy and kind here. I know because I have watched them. I have seen other chicken coops, and the hens there weren't kind to each other, they pushed each other around and pecked each other, stealing their food. Bad, really bad."

"You're right. The Hens are really nice, here, they share their food with us all the time." Stinky said, and both Reggie and Fernando agreed, nodding their heads.

"What do you think, boys?" Big Bird asked Stinky, Reggie and Fernando.

"Seems to me, the bloke is honest when 'e says 'es lonely." Reggie said, "maybe we should give the blighter another chance."

"No! Not another chance!" Fernando spat out. "How do we know he won't steal one of our Hens and run away with her?"

"Oh, no, I would never do that. I would wait for her, bring her flowers and mealy worms, until she wanted to be my love. I would never steal her. That would be so unkind, and unfair to her."

"He does have a point." Said Reggie, who was getting tired of sitting on the Hen Napper.

"What do you say, Fernando, should we give this bloke another chance? He sounds like 'e's a real gent." Reggie reasoned.

"I don't wish to hurt anyone." The Hen Napper said, "I will go away if you don't want me to stay here. I promise. Although I feel that my true love is here. I know that sounds like a hopeless romantic, but that is what I am. I just hide in the shadows so that no one can see my sad heart."

This last speech touched the boys. Stinky even wiped away a tear.

"Well, if you promise not to run away, I will ask the boys here to let you get up."

"Deal!" Said the Hen Napper readily, happy to finally get this large racoon off his chest and that sword point away from his neck. He had been extremely worried when they cornered him. He even had thoughts of becoming an angel far before his time. He waited to see what was to happen next.

Reggie rolled off the Napper's middle and Fernando sheathed his sword. The Napper stood and breathed a huge sigh, brushing his cape, and searching for his hat.

"What do you intend to do with me?" He asked.

"I'm not really sure, but we do have a party going on, and it is Christmas Eve." Big Bird thought a minute. "For the time being, you can come to our party, and we can figure it out in the morning, providing you don't try to escape."

"Deal!" for the second time.

Hen's Hangout

The Party

Fifteen Minutes Later

The Hen Napper A/K/A The Shadow

Chapter Twenty-Two

The party was slowly winding down. The presents
had been distributed by Santa Clacker, opened,
admired, and the wrappings cleared away.

Everyone was sitting or standing around, plates and drinks in hand, chatting happily to each other as the door opened again for the umpteenth time that night so that no one paid any attention to it until they saw who was standing there. A hush fell over the room: chatting stopped, eating stopped, drinking stopped, until there wasn't a sound. All the Hens in the room weren't certain who this dark stranger was. A few of the Hens stepped back cautiously away into the shadows.

The stranger stepped into the room, swishing his cape back over his shoulders. He removed his hat with a flourish and swept his sunglasses from his beaky nose. He scanned the room, one face at a time, until he stopped and stared at the face of Misty LaFogge (Comtesse Stephanie Felicite Brouillard).

He stared so long and so hard that her face feathers became a soft pink blush.

She fluttered her eyelashes.

He blinked his eyes.

She dropped her gaze.

He stared more intently.

She clasped her wings together to stop them from shaking.

He reached his wing out towards her hoping to touch her.

She looked up into his dark eyes.

He looked down into hers.

"Ma Cherie!" He murmured, reaching for her wing.

"Mon Ami!" She murmured, placing her wing in his.

Thunderous applause broke out throughout the Hen's Hangout. The room reverberated with clucks of happiness and well wishes.

He looked down at her and clucked softly, "Pour toujours et a jamais."

"Oui, pour toujours et a jamais!" She clucked softly in reply.

And so, Miracles Do Happen, even in Chicken Coops.

MEET THE CHICKS

In order of their appearance

Silver Laced Wyandotte

Tweetie Sweetie

Hi, I'm Tweetie, and I am a Silver Laced Wyandotte, a very pretty breed, if I may say so. Most of the time I am happy and out-going, because I do like to laugh! A LOT!

My very favorite thing is quilting. Why, you wonder, would a chicken want to quilt? Perhaps it is because the quilts, when finished are a beautiful piece of ART. So, you could say I am an artist only instead of paints, I work with material, a needle, and thread.

I am an avid reader, and have been since I was a baby chick. I always had a book hidden in my nest so my Momma Hen wouldn't find it. I do believe she knew, and approved. She was a reader, herself.

I had nine baby roosters in my family, so growing up was not easy. I did learn to help the other hens in the coop, and ran errands for them often. It was my way of avoiding my brothers. I didn't mind. I loved helping people, because it made them happy.

Here in the Coop, or the "Big House" some of the hens call it, I still help people. I'm in charge of our Coffee Clack, which meets weekly, and how this all started. I also help with the morning exercise, and trivia practice for the yearly Trivia Competition. I help organize games, a Book Club, and anything else we can think of that might be fun.

If you hadn't already guessed, I have a devoted admirer. Big Bird and I have been an "item" for thirty-five years. Someday we might get married. (Of course, we really are.)

NEW HAMPSHIRE RED

"Big Bird's my name and Chicken's my game."

I'm a handsome New Hampshire Red. Not a common breed, but of good solid stock. I watch over the Coop, and all the hens, in case they need a helping wing. You know what I mean, like taking out their trash, picking up their mail, giving them a ride when they need to leave the coop for an appointment.

I also like to do this because that way I can stay close to Tweetie (my) Sweetie. She is one gorgeous Chick, and I have eyes only for her! I even help her with her quilting for the holidays. Some of the items we make are for the other chicks in the coop.

I love to chat with everyone, which makes me out-going, Tweetie prefers to keep to herself, so we make the perfect pair. She probably already told you, "We are an item" and have been for thirty-five years. One of these days, I'm thinking I'll make an honest woman of her! Only joking! She is wonderful.

If you ever need aid or directions or anything that I can help you with, don't forget, "Big Bird's my name and Chicken's my game."

Frizzle Polish Hen

Fiona Frizzle

Hi Everyone. I'm Fiona Frizzle, the writer of this story. You can see from the photo that I am one of those Frizzled Polish Hens, although I have a completely different heritage. So much for the gene pool. I rather like the look, it is so – so – frazzled(?), anyhow I was dropped into the Coop from another similar coop but not at all as luxurious as this one. This one is a palace if we wanted to do a comparison.

Let me see, perhaps you would like to know how all of this started.

One day, during our weekly Coffee Clack, one of the hens remarked that we sounded just like a CHICKEN YARD.

We all agreed that she was correct, and that SOMEONE should write a story about us. (can you see the clue here?)

When all eyes turned to me, --- needless to say, tag, you are IT>

Now, I have never written a chicken story before so that was really stretching my literary talents, which were very - thin - to begin with.

There is a great deal more to this story, but perhaps we should save that for later. Suffice to say, here is the story so far.

Bon Jour, bon jour, my name ees Chicken-Little,

and I believe zat zee sky ees always going to

fall on us. It ees a senseless thing to worriee about it, becauuze eet may nevair happen, but then again, it might!

I am zee Silver Laced Wyandotte, zee same as zee Tweety-Bird, except I have zee feathers around my beautiful ankles. Did you not notice ziss?

I am zee quiet hen in zee Coop. I nevair say much of anything. I observe! Unless it izz about somezing dat will be dangerous, zen I scream, and yell, and shout! Dat izz only so dey will listen to me and hear what I say.

I adore les montagnes, especily zee French Alps, and Beethoven izz my favorite composer, comprenez-vous?

J'aime les chiens, et les enfants, et natomment la Famille.

To say I adore zee French Cooking would be silly, but of course J'aime pratiquement tout or Presque tout.

Blue Wheaton Ameraucas

Jollie- Joan

I go by the nickname, Jollie-Joan, I am a Blue Wheaton Ameraucas as you can see by my plumage. It is such a pretty color. My patients, when I was a nurse, always called me "The Blue Lady". I had the prettiest white lacy cap which I wore when on duty. I delivered baby chicks, and spent hours in the delivery room waiting for the chicks to hatch. That was such a wondrous experience.

I am the talkative one in the Coop. I have always been a clucker, since I was a baby chick. Good thing because it was useful in my career. As a nurse in the hatching room, you always had one or two nervous hens that didn't want to drop that egg, so I would talk them through it, and "pop" out it came.

Although that was a long-ago lifetime, now my days are spent with my "Cuddly Casey'. We walk side by side most days, regardless of the weather. Casey does love to dwaddle, though, and has helped me slow my pace the better to enjoy nature.

If we should hear of someone in need of nursing or nurturing, or sometimes just sensing that someone needs our help, Casey and I are always "on call". Remember, nurses are trained to be ready for any emergency or catastrophe. They always know exactly what to do.

Did I mention that Casey and I love to travel and have been to many places all over the globe.

Polish Frazzle Crested Hen

Goldie

Hi, I'm Goldie, the glamour girl of the coop, in case you haven't noticed. The photo does NOT do me any justice. I am far more glamorous in person. I spent ours in Clucks and Curls having my feathers 'done', and my wattles dyed an amazing RED. Originally, they are quite drab, and boring. (not at all like me).

My appearance belies my age, (which I won't reveal). I've always been taken for a much 'younger chick'. I guess it's the genes I inherited from my dear departed Mamma Hen, and her studley Roger Rooster – speaking of which – I have not given up on finding the perfect mate, one who appreciates a "wom-hen" of experience!

I love to perform – I sing (well, sort of) and dance from the first cock-a-doodle-do to the last owl's hoot. I am best known for the "CHICKEN DANCE" which I invented. (You didn't know that, did you?) Other imposters have tried to steal my thunder, especially at weddings, but when you see me strut my stuff, you are looking at the real deal.

That's about all I have to say about my fabulous self – I could go on for pages, but I'll leave room for others to have the spotlight. Just remember who's at the top of her game, and has been since she was a spring chicken.

BLUE ORPINGTON

SASSY SUE

Hello there,

My breed is a Blue Orpington, and we are a proud bunch of chickens. We do have some very strong opinions, perhaps that is why my name is 'Sassy-Sue'. My opinions are only a small part of me. I really am a very kind person, and will help anyone who needs it.

As a chick, I tend to keep to myself, although I do blend in with the other hens when we are together. The trickiest thing I must do when I am among the other hens is to remember to keep my opinions to myself, and only give them when I am asked. I believe that is a lesson that I need to learn. What is nice is the other hens do listen to what I say.

Aside from my 'sassiness', you can call on me to give help if anyone needs anything, from a ride to a concerned listening ear. Did I mention that I am very discreet?

Blue Polish Frizzle Chicken

Ms. Frazzle Dazzle

I know my name sounds like I would love footlights and center stage, BUT, I am extremely shy. I do prefer to be alone at times, and enjoy the peace and quiet.

My favorite thing is walking out in the sunshine with Missy. You will meet her later.

My nest is always neat and tidy, I dislike clutter, and get upset if my straw is out of place.

I have always been very sensitive, even as a baby chick, and used to hide under my Momma Hen's wing if someone made a joke about me, or anyone else.

Sometimes, when I'm trying to tell someone something, trying to cluck out my thoughts, I get excited and my clucks get loud so it sounds like I'm Clacking. The other hens understand, and they chirp their understanding when this happens.

My favorite thing, aside from walking Missy, is making people smile. I do so love to do that.

Well, Missy is here for our walk. See you later.

White Polish Frazzled Chick

Missy or Ms. Unpredictable

Hello. I'm Ms. Unpredictable, mostly known as "Missy". I am devoted to Ms. Frazzle Dazzle, and we walk everywhere, all the time.

I don't like some of the other chicks, especially the smaller ones, and they don't like me either. We Clack at each other, LOUDLY.

My best friend, Ms. Frazzle, tells me that I am sneaky and stubborn, but I'm not really. I just like my own way. When she wants to walk one way, I pull her wing so we can go the other way.

Some of my favorite things are visiting the other hens, preferably those without smaller chicks. Another thing I like is riding in a car with my head out the window. It feels so good fluffing my feathers.

Aside from that, my next favorite thing is mealtime and getting treats when I have been a good chick.

Sometimes, Ms. Frazzle takes me to the Big Coop and we do exercises together. Usually after that I am ready for a big sleep.

BLUE LACED RED WYANDOTTE

RUBY

My name is Ruby, and I have the ruby red feathers to prove it. They are pretty, aren't they? They are just like freckles, they never go away but they give one a certain characteristic, I think. Anyhow, that is why everyone calls me Ruby. I suppose it is better than Freckles.

All my chicken life, I have been a follower, never a leader. That is probably because I am inordinately shy. I do prefer quiet times to indulge in my passion for reading, not just any books, but my preference lies towards Historical Novels.

I dislike sports, and never played them growing up. I preferred my books, much to my parents' displeasure, as they envisioned me as a smashing tennis player. It was difficult to balance a tennis racket while my beak was stuck in a book.

Another thing, I HATE TO COOK. I would rather starve while reading a book, BUT, I do love sweets. That is how I survived all these years: A BOOK AND A BOX OF CHOCOLATES.

Black Polish Hen

Gadget

Hi, I'm Gadget. I'm a Black Polish Hen. Don't you just LOVE my beautiful plumage? I'm more at home in nature, and prefer to be out in the hen yard even after dark. You might find me prowling around in the moonlight or just sitting on a rock looking at the stars.

During the day, I love to sit quietly and listen to the sounds around me, or to just lie in the sun feeling its warmth.

I drive a black "Bug" and have travelled in it for many miles. We, the "Bug" and I love adventures, and have had many in our lifetime. Now we prefer to just still be in or near the Chicken Yard, although there are many places around here where we can go and explore.

I'm a recent resident in the Chicken Yard and have settled in nicely. The other hens have accepted my presence and have made me so welcome.

Well, I'm off to the beach, to scratch in the sand and to dabble my toes in the surf. Be back later. Hope to see you around, then.

Polish Frazzle Hens

SPIKE AND FLUFFIE

Spike has lived here for only a year. She came from the Cackle Hatchery where she spent years watching over the baby chicklings. She and Fluffie were married last year. Oh! What a celebration that was! Lots of dear friends from near and far attended. The Hen House was jumping that day!

Spike is an avid reader and enjoys films, especially Wonder Woman and The Minions. This year she tried to garden with Fluffie – not such a good idea – so now she is only allowed to do the watering.

Spike is kind and patient, and will also help others if asked.

Spike and Fluffie love to dance and listen to all kinds of music.

In their spare time, Spike likes to dabble with watercolors, and read (Spike prefers books, Fluffie devours the newspapers). They both watch HGTV informational channels on decorating and cooking, and are ready to help a friend any time they are needed.

Did we mention that Fluffie is a "Master Gardner"?

Gobble-dee-Cook

Hello, so nice to finally meet you. I don't get to visit except once a year. This year, the Hens in the Chicken Yard have kindly invited me for the holidays, my scariest time of the year. At least here, I will be safe and not end up in a very hot oven, and then on someone's table.

I did bring a small suitcase, so the Hens will understand that I do not intend to have an extended stay.

WHITE POLISH CHICKEN

Gorgeous Gladys

(G. G.)

Hi, my official name is Gorgeous Gladys, but the other chicks call me G. G. You can see by my picture, I am a White Polish Breed chicken. My head feathers are pure white and fluffy They weren't always that way. When I was younger, they were muddier brown and straight as a broom handle. I am a mom to four chicklets: two hens, two roosters.

My inner passion is making people laugh, being with my family and hanging out with friends. My other passions are dancing, (Jitterbug), beaching, (to lie in the sand and dip toes in the surf), reading, writing letters, and sending cards to friends. My creative expression is in my crocheting.

In the coop, I tend to be more of an observer sitting on the sidelines, but do enjoy the occasional company of other hens. I am spiritual, fun-loving, outspoken at times treat worthy, (candy please) and a good caring friend.

Hopefully, I am organized, but only in the most un-organized way.

Did I mention, I love CANDY, any kind, so long as its SWEET.

SPECKLED SUSSEX

LADY

Hi, my name is Lady, and I am a Speckled Sussex, as you can see by my beautifully colored feathers: claret and burgundy, laced with cobalt blue tipped with white. Striking in simplicity, aren't they?

I am an extremely quiet hen, more of an observer, than a participant. I adore being outside in the sunny fresh air.

During the cooler days, you might find me in my hen house watching the sports channel, particularly baseball. I love football and basketball. I played local league softball for many years until recently, when I retired.

I adore my chicken family, and have three of my own chicks, eight grand chicks, and six great grand chicks. There's safety in numbers, I always say.

I grew up with eight brothers, not an easy thing. I have two sisters, Margaret T. Hatcher, and Eggatha Christie. My sisters and I are very close.

Plymouth Rock Chicken

Breezy Brie

As you can see, I am a Plymouth Rock Chicken, with a very old heritage. I am an American Breed of Domestic Chicken. My breed was first shown in Boston in 1849. and for much of the early twentieth century was the most popular chicken breed in the United States. There are even Plymouth Rock breeders as far away as Australia.

I was born in Chatham and grew up here on the Cape, although some of my ancestors came from Canada. We are not a common breed any more but our numbers are rising. In my younger days, I laid over 200 eggs a year.

I prefer the quiet life, and enjoy the winter months, spent reading, writing poetry, playing my guitar, and cooking. Years ago, I wrote my own songs. Sports are not in vocabulary, neither is anything violent, an acceptable entertainment for others but not for me. My preferences tend more to knitting, sewing and the creative arts.

GOLD LACED POLISH CRESTED HEN

JUCIE JOYCIE or JJ

Hi All:

My name is Jucie Joycie, but most of the hens call me JJ. I like to think I am a caring and compassionate person, and I do like to have fun, because I know that is what life is all about. I am devoted to my family and friends. I like to be helpful and I am a very good listener.

When I am not here in the Hen House, I am volunteering somewhere, or sitting on a beach. (weather permitting, of course). Reading is another of my passions, and when I don't have my beak buried in a book, I am starting a new knitting project. I simply cannot sit around and do nothing, I love to stay busy.

Did I mention that I also like to do a little gardening if time and weather allow?

Polish Blue Frazzled Hen

Fancy Nancy

Hi, I'm Fancy Nancy, a Polish Blue Frazzled Exotic breed of chicken. I have recently returned from the SPA. I was there for four months after a fall off my nest which resulted in a broken hip. UGH! That was not fun.

At the SPA, I was treated with warm Epsom salts baths, which were so relaxing and helped my hip heal. They also changed my diet and fed me mealy worm sandwiches, and oyster shell salads swimming in olive oil, which were so delicious, I have no words to describe them. The best treat of all were the fresh veggies, lettuce, broccoli, kale, and beet greens.

It is so good to be back with my hen friends. I did miss them terribly.

Santa Clacker and Tinsel Tree

Ho, ho, ho, it's me again, that racy rooster from
the North. You may think I'm a dirty old man,
but I'm not. Under that red comb and white
beard beats a heart of pure love for all my
hens, and I have many. It is the perfect non-
committal relationship, because I only see them
once a year to bring them the present of their

dreams, which they request at the beginning of the month. In exchange, I get lots and lots of cookies and gallons of milk. It's like going to the food bank.

If I could make a small request? This year please leave double stuffed Oreos, they really taste good dipped in the milk.

The Hen Napper - The Shadow

Who knows what loneliness lurks in the hearts of hen-nappers?

The Shadow Knows.

I call myself "the shadow" because I am only a shadow of my true self. I am so lonely. I need someone to love and someone to love me. That is why I am trying to kidnap a chicken, so I will have someone to truly love. Chickens are always happy, clucking and preening their feathers. The hens in this coop seem to be the happiest I have ever seen, contented and friendly. Perhaps I can find my one true love here.

Pour toujours et a jamais. (Forever and ever).

I know! I am a hopeless romantic, but you see, I mean no harm to anyone. I am just a lonely shadow.

ACKNOWLEDGMENTS

We are deeply indebted to the 'Chicks' at POV III for their input, ideas, plots, and their patience as we designed and wrote this manuscript.

Special thanks to my writers at the Cape Cod Writers Studio who were my Beta Readers, and edited the contents of the book. They saw errors and grammatical mistakes I never knew existed.

Special thanks to Dave Clark from the group who threw out the title, which works perfectly.

We hope you enjoyed this book about Seniors who are impersonating Exotic Chickens who are impersonating Pin Cushions.

It is really about Seniors having fun!

The Chicks have requested a sequel. That may happen, there is certainly enough chicken feed to write about.

We have created a blog: Inside the Coop

Here is the link:

https://www.inside-the-coop.blogspot.com

Fiona Frizzle A/K/A

Sharon D. Anderson, PhD.

Fiona is an Author/Publisher, dedicated to her craft for more than 30 years. Most times, she writes in her Genre of Visionary Fiction, Non-Fiction, and sometimes in Fantasy bordering on Nonsensicality. (Fun).

She is a member of both the Cape Cod Writer's Center and the Visionary Fiction Alliance. She recently founded the Cape Cod Writer's Studio which meets weekly on Cape Cod, where she teaches members how to self-publish their work, supporting them on their paths to publication in the digital world.

She lives here on the Cape in the Coop.

Here is the link to her Amazon Authors Page:

https://www.amazon.com/author/andersonsharon

Tweetie Sweetie A/K/A

Candy Rogers

Tweetie is a Crafts Person/Artist, and has been drawing and quilting for most of her life. She creates unique and unusual projects and encourages the hens in the coop to bring out their creative abilities by making Seasonal Fairy Gardens, or cooking dishes for the potluck supper.

Tweetie is the Mother of the Hens in this coop. She organizes Trivia Practice, Book Clubs, Exercise Programs, Pot Luck Suppers, The Coffee Connection, Movie Night, Board Game Afternoons, anything that will motivate the Hens from their nests. She is the creator of the pincushions/illustrations for this book.

She lives with her husband Dave (Big Bird in the book) in the Coop.

Made in the USA
Columbia, SC
02 December 2017